THINGS WE TAKE,
THINGS WE LET GO

THINGS WE TAKE, THINGS WE LET GO

POEMS

CATHERINE MARENGHI

MADDALENA PRESS

WAREHAM, MASSACHUSETTS

Maddalena
Press

Cover Artwork: Kathleen Cammarata
Book and Cover Design: Mary M. Meade
Author Photo: Todd James McIntosh

First Edition
ISBN 979-8-9877442-2-2

To my mother, who never traveled far

Contents

From There to Here

My Books

Like loose hairs I brush from my head,
nail clippings, fluids and fingerprints
forensically identifiable
as traces of my body,
so are my books.

I couldn't keep them all
when I moved from there to here.

Some I've read from cover to cover,
others unread, but even so
they have comforted me
baring their lovely vertical spines,
a sentry of promises.

Yellowed paperbacks mixed
with cloth-bound hardcovers, many
still in glossy dustjackets. A few
in tooled leather, gilded lettering,
raised cords on the spines, only for show.

The ones I favored—poetry books,
the ones I will open again and again—
will stay with me till my eulogy
is sprinkled over my ashes.
Others I took only because
they were penned by my own hand.

Some 20 crates of books
traveled 2,600 miles with me.

The rest were dispersed to far-flung
library shelves, purveyors of used books,
Little Free Libraries. Stragglers
awaited new owners in boxes
left on my doorstep, marked
Free—please take.

The children's books, the ones
I once read to my son
were the hardest to part with.

But the ones that accompanied me
will be like a sourdough starter.
Wild yeast and ferment will
burgeon and blossom,
turning a single bookcase into
another house full of books,
shared like nourishing bread
passed from hand to outstretched hand.

Letters Tied With Kitchen String

Long after most of the world had phones,
my mother wrote letters.

And in return she received them,
kept them in bundles tied
with kitchen string, stuffed into
sticky bureau drawers, or her cedar chest
where they yellowed and crumbled,
waited for me to find them.

Some were birthday greeting cards
still holding crisp two-dollar bills—
silver certificates. Others hid checks
she never cashed.

And the news they shared
was never momentous.
A neighbor's child was starting school.
A recipe for gingerbread cake
copied from *Ladies' Home Journal.*
And always, how are the children?
Is Jerry working yet? Are you getting by?

A congregation of letters, receiving the day's gospel,
reciting it back. A polite call and response
on folded notes and cards a century old, not one
written by anyone still alive.

Will anyone find them precious but me?
Will anyone know who Aunt Ella is,
or Cousin George?

I will do today what someone else will do
when I'm gone: Stuff these letters into plastic bags,
toss them from my second-floor window
and into the dumpster below.

I'm sorry I can't take you with me,
Ella and George.
Or you, dear Mother.
I'm sorry.

The Needlepoint Sampler

My mother's needlepoint sampler
hung by her wood-burning stove for years,
glazed with cooking grease and dust.
You could barely make out the quaint
embroidered cottage, chimney cooing with smoke,
the pear tree cuddling close behind.

As a child, I thought it was our
house, but the Hollywood version,
editing out the sagging roof,
missing shingles. The outhouse
thoughtfully outside of frame.

I didn't appreciate it then,
the work of an unknown woman's hand
drawing the needle up through the linen,
down again, then up and across,
forming the tiny "x" stitches,
pixels of another era.

Years later I found it
cast aside in a damp cellar.
I pried the rusty staples loose
and rinsed the fabric, best I could,
stretching it taut between my hands
in soapy brown water, revealing the fine
cross-stitched letters:

HOME * SWEET * HOME

It will hang by another stove now
in my Mexican kitchen—
stitching my past and present together
in crisscrossing x's.

The Draper Badge

Employee badge number 3680.
Embossed tin.
Widely spaced letters
encircle its green rim.
DRAPER CORPORATION
once a maker of cotton looms,
now a relic of the smoky past,
fossilized like a woolly mammoth.

The green circle frames
my mother's face
as it was
before the man, the children,
the farm—ragged barefoot years,
leaving her feet and hands
chapped as elephant skin.

Before all that,
the girl who wore her future
like a gaggle of pin curls, clutched
her dreams as tight as the belt
cinched at her tiny waist.

Ever the good girl, doing her part
for the war effort, when
a maker of looms retooled,
did an abrupt about-face
to making howitzers.

Did she handle the metal parts, the barrels,
the casings? Hone projectiles that would tear
into enemy lines on the Guadalcanal?

When the war ended
she married the man
from the factory floor, the one who drove
the electric jitney, gave her a look
that scorched the line between
her past and her future.

She gave up everything for him, but this
she kept. Something he couldn't take from her.

A circular photo badge
like a coin in a vending machine
that slipped between the gears of time,
tumbled down her cedar chest
through sheaves of letters,
souvenirs and photos,
rolled to the bottom,
snagged in the sheer lingerie
she wore on her wedding night,
to find its home a lifetime later
in a satin jewelry pouch
in her daughter's Mexican home.

The Charlie Brown Lunchbox

A birthday gift to a little boy
in 1969.

Impossibly heavy metal box,
rounded corners,
toggle latch, a few dings
and grains of rust
on the orange trim.

Charlie Brown, Lucy, Linus,
Snoopy, Schroeder—comic strips
wrapped around the sides, like stories
circling a Grecian urn.

Inside a matching thermos
missing its red plastic cap.
This, its most endearing feature,
considering
it was he who lost it.

He who drank his chocolate
milk from it. He who loved it.
He who will always
be nine years old.

High-Heeled Shoes

It was madness to bring them
to San Miguel, where cobblestone streets
wage a bloody war against women
    in high-heeled shoes.

They call it the City of Fallen Women,
named for the tumble and pratfall
of those who dare step out
    in high-heeled shoes.

But mine were not just shoes.
They were works of art
sculpted in snakeskin, patent leather,
or suede, with flirty straps and buckles.
They gave my legs a suggestive curve,
and three or four inches of
elevation, making me statuesque
    in my high-heeled shoes.

Surely I'd wear them again.
If not in this Mexican town,
perhaps on my trips to the States,
for galas, receptions, calling for dressy
    high-heeled shoes.

I imagined a TV talk show host,
beckoning me to the guest chair,
where I would sit and seductively fold

my leg, flashing my perfectly beautiful
     high-heeled shoe.

But I have traveled time and again,
and carried only my
practical footwear, flats,
sneakers, kitten heels, but never
     high-heeled shoes.

I was warned of the dangers,
musculoskeletal injuries, bunions,
swollen feet, plantar fasciitis,
arthritic pinch and pain
     from high-heeled shoes.

Yet here they are. Perched in neat rows
on my closet shelves, as if caressing
the feet of invisible women,
waiting to walk down an aisle to a son's
wedding, command an executive suite,
or step out onto a dance floor.
They stand in judgment of my vanity,
receptacles of a younger woman's fantasies,
     these high-heeled shoes.

I choke on the words "younger woman."
Perhaps it is down to this:
I have to admit I am past the age
     for high-heeled shoes.

Leaving Massachusetts

Before the maple leaves have a chance
to set themselves on fire again, and
summer has ticked off its annual checklist:
     Day lilies—done.
     Irises—done.
     Hedge roses, lavender, blackberries—done.
That's when I haul the suitcases down from the attic.
Check the date on my passport. Pull up weather reports
to see what's falling from Mexican skies.

The cat will miss you, my brother says.
But I know what he means.
We who have six decades behind us
don't need to belabor good-byes. He
was always the rooted part
of our family tree, and I
the wind-borne seed.

Leaving Massachusetts has been habit-forming.
Its airport knows me well enough
to leave the key under the doormat.
I've grown weary of the weather's mood swings,
from the scolding tongue of February
to September's sycophantic praise.
The backhanded slap of its summer sun
has reddened my cheek more than once.
I say I won't return, but something
always turns me around.

What is it about this bay state
that stretches its scrawny arm
into the wild Atlantic
to beckon me homeward?
Every peak and pillar here
is saturated
with something remembered—
the first time I sang, or walked, or loved,
or grieved, or bore a child,
my first of every
everything
was always here.

All That Is Heavy

The house had to be staged and decluttered
before it went up for sale.

I filled box after corrugated box
with non-essential things.
That is to say, all of my things.

I crammed the boxes into my car,
chauffeured them like VIPs
to a storage locker, a dozen trips,
feeling for once the enormous weight
of all I owned,
the physical burden
straining and curving my back
like a bentwood chair.

I had become a sherpa
for things,
loading them onto the dolly
rolling them down the maze
of fluorescent halls
to my numbered storage compartment
stacking the boxes six high
and ten deep
and still they were greedy
craving ever more space.

I'm reminded of the Salem witch trials
where one of the accused was

laid under boards, and heavy rocks
were piled on top, one by one, until
he was slowly crushed to death.

I can't imagine what makes me think of this.

The Antique Singer Sewing Machine

Weighing more than a person,
it would never make the cut
for the *menaje de casa,*
essential household goods
specially chosen, labeled, and packed
for shipment to Mexico.

The Singer Model 127, made to last
a hundred years,
with darkly varnished cabinet,
original belts and bobbins, black
wrought-iron stand and treadle,
handwheel still spinning smoothly
as if it were freshly oiled.

No one then had ever conceived
of planned obsolescence. Instead
they built this lovely machine
with paisley flourishes
laced with gold and feminine swirls
to be handed down from mother
to daughter, back when they thought
the world would never end.

Nothing is made like this anymore.

Here, I will hand it off to you,
and please don't tell me
you've painted it red or some

god-awful color, turned it into a lamp,
or left it out in your garden to weather,
a whimsical artifact on which
to arrange your flowerpots.

Let me imagine you instead
as a diligent seamstress,
working into the night:
slanted eye, steady hand,
your feet gently rocking the treadle,
forming a perfectly straight seam.

The Affair

When my Massachusetts house
saw me packing my bags for Mexico,
she began to suspect, but then
she is old and very wise.
How many times
has she counted my lovers' footsteps
on her creaking pumpkin-pine stairs?
She misses nothing.

I could feel her disapproving eyes
from afar,
as I stood on a San Miguel street
admiring the fine bones of a much
younger house.

Its lithe arched iron windows
cast mosaics of curved light
on polished Cantera floors.
Lemon-tree bouquets in the courtyard
wooed me. Clinging bougainvillea
kissed me hard
with lipstick blossoms.

When I returned to my old house,
she could sense my treachery.

You've allowed strange men to come,
she said. *They box my bangles and trinkets,*

You want one in every port!
she accused.
But no, I confessed,
I want only one:
the house in San Miguel.

At this she felt such rage
she began to will herself
to rot at her sills,
clenched her roof shingles
till they swallowed the rain
and stained her plaster ceilings.

You will pay for this, she said.
No one will want me now.

Possums

What did I really leave behind?
The job that paid well
and cost me dearly?
        Every day an act of suicide
        that I survived
        only to do it again
        day after day.

What do we want to leave behind?
        The lovers who disappointed us?
        Is it better to be alone
        Or not alone?
        Either one can kill you.

What do we ever leave behind?
        We carry our regrets,
        suspicions and miseries
        like baby possums
        on their mother's back.
        Nothing ever lets go, does it?
        The same voices screech in the night,
        but also the loves we carried.
        All of them hang on hopefully,
        and hopelessly.
        Every move a stepping stone
        that disappears, swallowed up
        as the earth gives way behind us.

A New Country

Reveille

The first thing you learn about San Miguel
is the roosters.
They don't crow at first light.
They crow and they crow
whenever they crow.

And the church bells are not
like the ones I remember, evenly spaced
peals from precise Bostonian steeples.
No, they're more like tin
spoons, banging on cast-iron skillets,
calling *vaqueros* home for their supper.
They clang and they clang
whenever they clang.

And the dogs, barking up on the rooftops—
What are they doing up there, chained
to the sun, and not at their masters' feet?
One dog's barking sets off the next
like an endless string of firecrackers.

To say nothing of the grackles—
Loud, strutting, arrogant black
sheen, their screeching fills in the blanks
between the barking, crowing, and clanging,
a popping, grinding mess of sounds,
layered over and under each other,
like terracotta tiles on the rooftops,
waking me up from my gringo sleep.

Let me, then, shake off all my northern clocks
like dust rising from cobbled streets
after a sudden rain. Let me join
the murmuration of starlings,
swaying to this impossible chorus,
adding my own faint chirping sounds,
the shy quarter note of grief, the half note
of longing.

Let me rest my yawning head
on this wild disheveled place, a newborn babe
on her mother's shoulder, limp and yielding.

Do not wake me. Do not wake me at any
particular hour.

Mexican Crickets

They huddle under the door jam,
where it's moist and dark.
They think it's night. Wings ridged
like baby teeth rub together. Shrill
echoes skitter across the tile floors,
the male cricket's wolf whistle
to his soft-spoken mate.

The chirping lifts my stucco house
from its foundation, carries it over
the Gulf of Mexico, as if borne
by the blessed Virgin of Loreto
northward to Massachusetts,
backward in time, plunking it down
by the muddy frog pond
of St. Mary's Cemetery,
rank primordial swamp that brewed
life as I first witnessed it:
dragonflies with glass wings, big-headed
tadpoles finding their first feet, water lilies
floating like long-tentacled jellyfish, and
always, as the evening fell, that chipper
cricket mating call.

I wade across my living room
knee-deep in memory, slick as mud.
The years fall away like dew-covered
spiderwebs in my path.

Citizen

I want to be one of the SanMiguelenses.
No more *turista*. No *voyeurista*.
No more stopping to photograph.
Barely pausing at bougainvillea.
Turning away from the bosom of golden
loaves at the *panadería*. Snubbing the frilled
skirts of the *calabaza* blossoms. Shunning the
pursed lips of the pomegranates.

Like a former lover you pass on the street,
pretending not to see, nothing will shake
my forward gaze. Not if I wish to blend in,
as one adobe brick among many.

Only when a street vendor calls me *güera*,
offers a fringed *rebozo* held like a matador's
fiery cape, I snap back into my *gringa* skin,
surrender my ever-widening eyes
to the Otomi women in pleated skirts,
their necks ringed with straw beads
for sale, the mother and son
hawking whittled wooden burros,
and Carlos balancing dozens of straw hats
in a single stack on his head. That's when I
dig deep in my pockets for pesos
to buy a Mariachi song.

Spanish Lessons

You learn there are two words
for "to be":
ser and *estar.*
The latter implies
a transitory state, as in
está feliz—he is happy,
just for the moment.
But they also say *está muerto*
as if death were a mere pause
in life eternal.
Our country is Catholic,
my teacher tries to explain.
And yet they say *Ojalá*—
God willing—a word
plucked from a Muslim god.

But here's what gets me:
The same word—*historia*—
means both history and story,
one of them true,
one of them not.

The same word—*esperar*—
means both to wait and to hope.
Presumably one who waits
is one who hopes,
and one who hopes
is one who must stand and wait.

Yellow Moons in My Hands

Bright moon, not quite full, hovers over skylights
casting parallelograms of light on red Saltillo floors.
I rise from bed, thinking there's a prowler on the roof
training a flashlight beam on my bedroom floor.
I stare upward to the light, seeing only the moon's
yellow face. Strange, how the moon seems not to move,
and yet it stirs the pot of roiling ocean tides, pulls
and tugs the hair of clouds.

I move through dark rooms throwing windows open.
A western wind rolls in across the Sierra Madres,
blows its hot dusty breath on the slender necks
of lemon trees. Tomorrow when the grackles screech
at first light, I'll gather the Meyer lemons scattered
over the courtyard, before the garden snails can scar
their tender skins. I roll the fruit between my hands,
breathe in their scented oil, like small yellow moons.

Gardener's Plot

Dust and desiccation
dreck and deadwood
courting atrophy,
tributaries narrowing,
a womb bled out,
walls and membranes
stretched to breaking,
skin taut and clenched
into a self-embrace
incapable of need.

And from that came
green restored
by drench and drink,
perfect furrows
lined up like schoolchildren,
eager and obedient,
guided by your
weathered hands.

You turned and worked
the hardened soil,
dug deep enough
to find a fan of roots
fine as baby hair,
coaxing them to reach up
through dark and dirt
to be astonished by
the morning sun.

The Swallow of San Miguel

You, down there, earthbound artist
in your plein-air studio,
I see you try to copy
nature's perfect canvas
as a poor stenographer
with shorthand lines and strokes.
You'll never master it,
but I applaud the effort.

Call me *golondrina*.
You know me by my tail,
forked like an arrow's fletching.

I sense that you admire me, but
you only see my form.
You do not know me.

I am not a thing of air and feather.
I am solid, deadly as
an arrow shaft, my beak aimed
at fluttering prey,
my pale breast a dinner napkin
tucked beneath my chin
as I feast in flight. My banquet is
the evening sky.

You add me as a mere
embellishment to grace
your verdant canvas, with

succulents, aloe flower,
rare hibiscus, frangipani,
all arranged to frame my own
curvaceous flight.

You think me only for the eye?
You who swept away
my nest, offended by my droppings,
even though I inhabited your portico
long before you bought the house.
I had the better claim to it.

I watch you thrash and swat
and never catch a single gnat or fly,
while I devour them by the dozen.

Let me strike a deal with you.
I will leave my droppings
as a gift to you, a love note
in the style of Jackson Pollock,
telling you
I've come to stay.

I'll be good to you.
I will clear your nest
of buzzing, biting things
while I restore my own
pretty nest,
my cool mud-lined walls.

Let me live at your side,
not as artist's model,

but as teacher, you as my apprentice.
Let me help you see
what I can see.

I Seem to Take a Lot of Pictures
of Flowers Lately

I favor extreme closeup shots, nearly falling into the
calla lily's chalice. Creamy spathe enwraps the spadix,
jutting popsicle stick that's studded with tiny
orange flowers you can't see unless you look closely.

I see flowers everywhere, the daily Rorschach test
of crumbling stucco walls, clusters of color
fallen away, leaving wounds of odd shapes, and
I choose to see a spray of chrysanthemums,
white as salt.

I understand the flowers are a form of escape.

Just as I stare out the window of an airport shuttle van,
my eyes trying to gather the flowers blurring past
on the Mexican desert, my body turned to avoid
conversation with the *gringo* seated next to me,
spouting off how much he loves the man
in the White House, the one with skin
the color of marigolds.

I try to imagine a trellis between us, covered with thorny
vines, and I lose myself in the nopal cactus flanking
the highway. As if waiting for a parade, they wave their
paddle hands and wear their sunbonnets studded with red
prickly pear. The *gringo* beside me sees them, too.
The prickly pear! he exclaims. *Don't they look like red roses?*

And suddenly the trellis between us disappears.
Our conversation turns to gardening.

Is this all that's required, then, to look more closely?
Spathe and spadix, micro blooms that barely graze the eye.
Petaled ambassadors of goodwill that draw us closer,
asking only that we narrow the lens for a closeup shot.

Ofrenda del Día de los Muertos

I never used to like to visit cemeteries.
Voiceless graves. No one really there.

Mexico taught me that
the dead return to visit us,
not to haunt,
but gently keep us company,
to reminisce.

You lay out their favorite foods,
sugar skulls, incense, and marigolds.
Their photographs.

You think about
the things they loved
and then
they are at your side.

Never do they overstay their welcome.

Cockscomb Seeds

Bouquets of shaggy cockscomb
bought for *Día de los Muertos*
scattered tiny seeds like ground pepper
on my table linens.

I gathered all the seeds with care,
planted them in starter pots,
anticipating lush red waves of coiling
sea coral. What emerged instead
was one tomato seedling.
A sneaky stowaway.

I don't know what happened to the
cockscomb seeds. I so hoped
for them to work as hard as I did
to take root in fresh foreign soil,
and bare their red velvet crests
bursting from their stems
like the heads of roosters.

Pantoum for the Unknown Soldier

—From a news report in the San Miguel Herald, Mexico

Just after dawn, gunshots fired at the entrance to Taboada.
Police at the scene reported a white Chevy pickup truck.
A man inside was wearing a checkered shirt,
denim pants, and five gunshot wounds.

When police arrived at the scene, a Chevy pickup truck
was wearing white paint and a blood-red interior.
A man inside wore denim pants, and five gunshot wounds.
The uniform of a drug war's unknown soldier.

With white paint on a blood-red canvas,
the United States of America writes its name.
The uniform of a drug war's unknown soldier
leaves a trail of blood to your golden door.

The United States of America signs its name
when gunshots shatter the dawn at Taboada.
A trail of blood runs to your imported guns
from five purple hearts pinned to the unknown warrior.

The Bus to Chichicastenango

Leaving Panajachel
staring out through tinted glass
the passengers eye the town
that speeds away behind them.

Rusted corrugated roofs,
flowers grown in tin cans
and pink plastic pails,
yellowed plastic tape over
long-broken windows.
Paint and weather-bleached posters
peeling off stucco walls
like curling leaves
leaning to the sun.

One passenger sees
a swirl of trash, a prison
made of cinderblock,
a Third World,
a festering, a slum.

Another tourist sees
sweet chaos, authentic life
without forced aesthetics,
bougainvillea climbing
where it pleases,
meager backyard *milpas*
that fed generations,

dried cornstalks
waving golden tassels
to the passing bus
like a flock of pale
flitting birds.

Chicatanas in Rainy Season

Flying ants tumble like amber blossoms
shaken loose from trees after the
first June rains in San Miguel. Their wings
stick to wet pavement, beaded bodies
crushed under passing cars.

Having completed their nuptial flight,
the males resign themselves to death,
nothing left for them to do
while females bore underground
to birth their colonies, chewing off their own
wings to feed their young.

Which would I choose?
The rapid crashing flight of death?
Or sure-footed, prolonged labor
of earthly home?

I know the answer.
Wing stumps still blister and burn
as I will myself to grow them back.

Unattached

Papel picado banners flutter over
the courtyard, fountains spit
from the mouths of sculpted fish,
and grasping trumpet vines
litter the pavement tiles with
puckered blossoms.

It's best to be alone sometimes.
To hear no utterance but the
buzzing wings of hummingbirds.
Nothing to drown the whisper
of the pages flipping from poem
to poem, a favorite book out-
stretched on my lap like a yawning cat.

Today I will not surrender myself,
dive headlong into other people's
chattering lives, giving up the sureness
of my own private moorings.

Today my door is bolted against
any knock or chime. Faintly I hear
human voices tossed like trash
from passing cars, carried away
on the rumors of the wind.

Credits

"Leaving Massachusetts" was previously published in the fall 2019 issue of *Peregrine Journal.*

"The Affair" received first prize in poetry at the Marblehead Festival of the Arts, Marblehead, MA, 2018.

"Reveille" was published in the 2017 edition of *Solamente en San Miguel,* an annual anthology of poetry and fiction inspired by San Miguel de Allende, Mexico.

"I Seem to Take a Lot of Pictures of Flowers Lately" appeared in *Conclave,* Balkan Press, Spring 2019.

"Mexican Crickets" was published in *Ruminate!* Issue 60, fall 2022, under the title "Crickets."

Acknowledgments

This book is a contemplation on transition and change. It centers on a life-altering move to a new country, a destination that was never in my plans. But one day it became my only plan.

In February 2014 I attended the San Miguel Writers' Conference in San Miguel de Allende, Mexico. It was a week that still holds me in place, fixes me in time like a pushpin to the calendar.

Before then, I had never heard of either the town or the conference. I went there on a friend's suggestion, little more than a whim.

I was 59 years old. I had lived in Massachusetts all my life. My only child had recently graduated from college. I was still working full-time in the corporate world, but I was thinking ahead. I had started spending my weekends and vacations attending writers' conferences and retreats, hoping to reawaken a long-deferred passion for writing.

Something happened in San Miguel. A feeling of happiness and well-being flooded over me. Yes, the town is beautiful, and the weather is lovely. But it was something else. I felt alive. I felt young.

I attended the conference three years in a row before realizing I could not return to my old life in Massachusetts. I sold one house and bought another.

This book gratefully acknowledges the influence San Miguel
has had on my creative life. The friends, writers, and artists I
have encountered here have inspired me, shaped my writing,
and propelled me to publish five books in eight years.

It was here that I met and learned from extraordinary poets
and teachers like Richard Blanco, Sandra Cisneros, Jennifer
Clement, Judyth Hill, and many other exceptional writers.
I wish to extend particular thanks to Kathryn Jordan, a fine
poet whose insightful questions and smart comments on this
manuscript were invaluable.

—Catherine Marenghi

About the Poet

Catherine Marenghi is an award-winning poet, memoirist and novelist. Her poetry books include *Unfurled: Love Poems* (2023), of which Sandra Cisneros said, "Here is poetry written from the exquisite perspective of a woman of a certain age"; *Breaking Bread: Poems* (2020), a book about family, love, and the endless longing for home; and now this latest collection, *Things We Take, Things We Let Go.*

She is also the author of *Our Good Name* (2022), an historic fiction based on her Northern Italian immigrant ancestors; and *Glad Farm: A Memoir* (2016), a story of stark poverty and resilience, set on a former gladiolus farm in Massachusetts. President Jimmy Carter called her memoir "inspiring."

Among her poetry awards, she received first-place honors in separate poetry contests judged by acclaimed poets Richard Blanco and Jennifer Clement. Her poems also twice received first-place honors from the Academy of American Poets university poetry prize program and received a Yeats Poetry Prize honorable mention. Her poetry has been nominated for the Pushcart Prize.

Catherine's writing has appeared in such international journals as *Cider Press Review, Sisyphus, Peregrine Journal, Bangalore Review, Ekphrastic Review, Italian Americana, Phi Kappa Phi Forum, High Shelf Press, Solamente en San Miguel, Mobius, Ruminate, Wingless Dreamer,* and *Conclave.*

She holds an M.A., B.A. summa cum laude in English from Tufts University, where she studied with poets Denise Levertov and X.J. Kennedy. She is active in the rich literary community of San Miguel de Allende, Mexico.

She currently divides her time between Massachusetts and Mexico.